SHE'S MAGIC

&

MIDNIGHT LACE

She's Magic
&
Midnight Lace

a collection of dark poetry & poetic spells

ANN MARIE ELEAZER

300 SOUTH MEDIA GROUP | NEW YORK

ISBN-13: 978-0-9970356-9-8

First Printing November 2021

Published by 300 South Media Group

Praise for Ann Marie

Poetry, simply said, is her magical potion.
Darkened and mysterious words form deep within her old
soul, executed with pinpoint precision as she lulls her
audience into a hypnotic trance.

Ann Marie's poetry, with a hint of Poe sprinkled to and fro,
brings life to those obscure hidden desires of yesteryear.
With a hint of mystery, a dash of seduction and wording that
seemingly dances in unison,

Ann Marie's arrangement of words casts a bewitching spell
upon those that dare transcend into her magical coven of
poetry.

Maxwell Xavier,
Writer at Primal Awakenings

This poetry sings to deep hidden places in my heart,
allowing me to embrace my own wild and beautiful
darkness.

If you yearn for a sensual life, shun pastels and feel at home
in mysterious places, you will love this book.

I read it to my lover late at night and watch it bring out his
inner wicked passion.

Elisa Robyn, PhD,
Author of The Way of The Well and Dark Fire

TABLE OF CONTENTS

POEMS & POETIC SPELLS

Dedicated to my greatest loves, Jade & Sage; who are my biggest inspiration; who taught me the meaning of unconditional love and that dreams can, indeed, come true.

To the enchanted Mystic woods that helped raise me, and the fairytale witches who showed me what life can be like when the princess doesn't win in the end.

Her Darkness

A woman's darkness is graceful.
It wraps around her like a silk dress
and breathes thunder into her alter ego.
It holds close her smirks & sorrows,
and is her most loyal playmate.
On stormy nights,
you can hear her chimes blowing in the wind.

Inky Elegance

She wasn't made for spring or splendor.
She glows in edginess and erotica...a bit of inky elegance.
Lips afire in blood and bedtime stories.
A strange and wicked moon.

Mad Tea Parties

While other little girls were on the playground,
she was in the forest having mad tea parties
with the fairies, critters, and crows.

The Best of Them

Even on my best days,
I can still feel the wings
of a thousand crows
flapping inside of me.

Dark Queens

While they were drawn to the glitter,
princes and heroic rescues,
my eyes fluttered to the haunted forests...
the swish and sway of the Dark Queen's gown,
and the way the ravens perched
atop the evil castle at midnight.

Bloom

Some women bloom pretty in pink
while others grow wild vines in vivid,
somber shades of slate.
A deep breath of the pages to her favorite book,
erotic fairytales and venom.

Be Careful

Be ever so careful when dancing in her garden,
for she blooms in baby's breath,
belladonna,
wolf's bane
and bleeding hearts.

Villain's Dark Kiss

My heart is insatiable for those arousing, drowsy love stories.
The ones dressed in drenched skin and feverish sobs.
But my soul, shrouded in beds of black dahlias
and hidden fortresses,
will always crave the villain's dark kiss.

Otherworldly

The way midnight settled in her eyes
and danced through her hair,
you would think she was an otherworldly creature
or a dark fairytale waiting to be told.
Maybe she was...

Dusk & Dawn

Her soul breathes a sigh of relief between dusk and dawn.
In the quiet, shadowy slumber of night,
her secret garden blooms
and her imagination climbs longingly
out of the rabbit hole.

Witchy, Wicked Little Thing

Oh, those dark, whimsical ones.
A little enticing.
A little elusive.
Her heartstrings will hypnotize you,
while the chanting of her poetry
haunts you to hell and back.

Her Arrival

She arrives in a vintage carriage of darkness
like the forbidden side of the castle
and the hungry side of the moon.
The part of the forest they warned us about
and lovers who arrive too soon...
(with no warning, booming thunder, pelting rain on an
unsettled evening in June).

Wild Orchids

She has a dark, vintage soul
where black butterflies dance
and wild orchids grow.

Skeleton Bows

I always preferred the forest to the playground;
moonlight to sunlight.
Skeleton bows, magic and winds that blow...
and those dark lullabies
singing to the black roses that follow her to and fro.

Haunted Ruins

Midnight girls,
Smelling of thunder and ink;
of falling in love and haunted ruins.
Of brewing storms, black lace thighs and things that fly.
Of him and I.

Madman's Love Song

For they were the Dark Maidens;
the madman's love song....
intense, witchy and shadowy;
wicked and opulent.
Men wonder if they had been
poisoned or doused in her nectar.

Black as Pitch

She's all black...
her thoughts,
her moods,
her words,
her scent
and her closet full of
pretty little darkness.

The Nightingale's Trill

Some women are shades of blush and princess
with singing bluebirds and touches of silk.
While women like me are shades of sable and witch,
with a nightingale's trill and touches of ornate lace.

Book Dragon

She loved brooding men;
curling up at night to play make believe with
Heathcliff, Mr. Darcy & Dracula.
She also loved to slip into darkness and surrender to
the creatures under the moon.
Her dark layers were endless.

𝕸aleficent 𝕲irls

The ones born with fairy blood,
who dance with their darkness
and roam quiet places conversing
with crows and clouds.

Bite Marks

And for those of us like Maleficent,
dark souls and hazel eyes
seeking things that hide in the night,
true love's kiss never comes easy.
But when it does,
it's accompanied by the whispers of dead poets,
who sing mad love songs
and leave bite marks behind.

Let's Go to the Opera

She's...
Dancing lady orchids,
death's murmur
and
a nocturnal opera.
She has a thing for playing with fire.
Enticed by poison apples and wild creatures
concealed as sparkling charms.
Silken vows that turn to stone.

Isolation

All I want is to be an isolated Queen...
giant thorns guarding my forest; fairies, ravens
and enchanted creatures as confidants.
And to cast evil spells on fools and foes
while draped in black elegance.
Is that too much to ask?

Dust

She may have a vintage heart
veiled in dust and darkened clouds,
but her soul is bursting in
fire and full moons.
You can find her up past her bedtime
perusing forbidden places
and playing with things that don't belong to her.

Her Wings

You can try breaking her wings,
but as forever shows
she always has another pair preened and ready to go,
for a girl and her familiar are an endless love affair.

Whoever She Wants to Be

She was a little bit Lilith and a little bit Eve,
and she was tired of people telling her
who the fuck she should be.

Fairytales (Need Girls who are More)

Enchantress
Sorceress
Poetess
Temptress
Huntress
      & less
Princess

Made for the Dark

She was made for the dark...
the magic;
intimate feasts with wolves;
steamy fairytales;
full moons
and that old Hollywood romance with men
who dressed gentle, but loved rough.

Arm Her

Arm a woman with your
loyalty, love and longing
and she will not only walk with you once upon a dream,
but she will make that dream come true.

Wolf & Witch

He was the wolf to her witch,
the temper to her tantrums
and the hand that softly led her down portals of hell
while both of them begged for more.

Velvet Eyes

I don't want soft lips or pretty boys on white horses
I want sharp teeth that sink into my soul
Men in black capes
Mad-mannered werewolves
Beasts and velvet eyes.

Magical Scent

Be careful when you breathe her in...
Her holy, immortal and magical scent
will bring out the madman in you.

Sleepy Towns

I want to happen upon a sleepy town with hollows
and handwritten confessions.
Enchanted hamlets,
scarlet sins and beasts on black stallions.
A place tucked away from reality
where the clouds collect
and my wildflowers grow under the moon.

Shades

She blushed of sin and serenity,
longing for a man to bring her both.
Linked fingers in moments of silence
and gritty, addictive nights laying spent.

Dark Minds

It's not the Disney ever after magic I crave.
It's darkness and solitary moors,
ravens reciting nevermore
and the way
his dark mind winks at mine.

𝕻𝖑𝖆𝖙𝖍 & 𝕻𝖔𝖊

Don't bring me roses.
Bring me Plath & Poe,
bouquets of black pansies
and nights filled with thunder and sweat.

Horn & Halo

Some women are more halo than horn
and hellfire than holy water.
Some have a bit of heaven and a dash of hell.
And when you find the one with a perfect blend of all,
hold on and never let go.

𝔐istress

She's...
The raven's playmate,
evening rain lilies
and a villain's mistress.
Always drawn to those spooky ruins' types;
dark castles upon a hill, ominous and alone.
Like a verse in the middle of a sad song
waiting to be understood...
waiting to be loved for exactly who they are.

𝔑𝔢𝔳𝔢𝔯𝔪𝔬𝔯𝔢

Some girls get lost amongst fairytales
and stories of ever after,
while others find themselves pressed between the pages
of horror and heartbreak
and dreams not of this lifetime.

Mad Girls

Give me the strange souls
and the moonstruck,
the mad girls
and the misunderstood.
The ones who play in the dark
and live with one foot dancing
with Hemingway and Poe.

Poet's Soul

It's always fair in love and war, fairytales and nevermore.
But hardly in the way his love seeped into my veins
by way of poison
and the tragic sounds of his poet's soul.

Twins

~Dark Queen~
Quick tempered, deep merlot thoughts,
black-tinged lips; sooty love stories;
swirling eyes and a hauntingly wispy heart.
Not for the faint and feeble.

~Emerald Maiden~
Emerald forests, mossy moods,
jade-filled dreams, solemn,
velvety sage kisses and veins that grow
spider mums.
Not for the meek and mild.

Don't you Dare

Never underestimate the power
of a woman's spirit animal.
She's more than a pretty face or satin and lace.
She's the roar of the night and the kiss of sparrows.
Intuitive whispers and eyes that know.

Her Abyss

Scarlett's temperament
Sylvia's heart
Dracula's thirst
A haunted love song.
She'll surrender her soul
while sending you into her abyss.

Pretty Collector

Nothing haunts me more than the ravenous creatures
I've collected along the way.
An enchanted assortment of darling,
dangerous and downright indifferent.
Some days they help me adorn my crown,
while others we visit hollow ground.

Those Eyes

Maybe that's a twinkle in her eye...
or just her dragon ready to play.
But, beware.
If you don't unlock her doors
and set her thoughts on fire,
you're not the one.

Wilting

There's beauty in the wilt of her eyes
the rain in her skies
the thorns in her sides
the cloud cover over her heartstrings.
The way she plays in the dark,
tangles herself up in bouquets of long-lost memories
and old books collecting dust on hidden shelves...
things often left behind.

Buried Treasure

She's buried treasure and a rainy-day girl, darling.
Full of storms and sin;
blue lavender
and the temper of a thousand sea witches.
If you can't stand the deep end,
stay out of her darkness.

Temptress

I'll always be a temptress for things that haunt me.
That steal my breath, bewitch me & break my heart...
feral, forsaken.
Things buried, but still alive.

Pleasure Never Tasted So Good

Her fangs will bring you far more pleasure
than her lips ever will.
Like a soft midnight
and a stormy morn.
Lustrous eyes and ripened berries,
biting rain and a dark kiss.
You'll want her, but need her so much more.

Chamber Doors

If you decide to open up my chamber door,
don't say I didn't warn you.
The haunting wolf melodies and pitch-dark affection
may lull you to sleep forever.

Dark Side of the Clouds

She's no spring pea or summer dahlia.
She's autumn leaves, earthy and enchanting;
and winter's frost, with a hint of opaline and howling wind.
Always on the dark side of the clouds.

Drowsy Love

A lady who loves romantic kisses,
rough touches under the moon,
and naughty words
falling from drowsy lips upon her skin.

Doe–Eyed

He was a lover of dark things,
doe-eyed demons and dragons.
Lucky for him she was all three.

Rainy Days

Rainy days cast a spell on my soul,
daring me with the way they sink their teeth into my soul
with the strength of a lover's bite
and the soothing sensation of his kiss.

Silk & Satin

She's a mad one;
a wildflower...
all silk thorns and satin teeth.
A bewitching beauty in a dark novel
that keeps you up in the middle of the night.

Weaknesses

I have a weakness for feral hearts
and rough edges disguised as silk.
Like a wild rose bashfully peeking through
the cracks of an ancient Gothic ruin,
I ever so delicately bloom through his mind,
daring his darkness to claim me.

Defiantly Different

I love vintage souls with peculiar habits
and that faraway look in their eyes.
Different...so beautifully, defiantly different.

That Energy

My, how the energy and the attitudes in the room change
when her darkness shows up.
Most fear it will bite them,
but she's more loving than her heart & soul combined.

Kingdoms by the Sea

She played house in cloudy castles
and shared secrets with the crows.
And while mother read her happily ever after,
she dreamt of kingdoms by the sea
and the dark love of Poe.

Dark Goddess

She's no doll, no Snow or Cinder...
She's Edgar's Annabel,
Clyde's girl
and the Crow's keeper.

Her Castle

Every woman has a castle.
Some are brimming in glint and gold,
while others are filled with shadow and secret.
Hers is beautifully abandoned, secluded and silent,
laced with diaries of erotic-like mystery
and love gone astray.

Solitude

Some days I long for complete solitude;
a forest cave, with nothing but the sounds of silence
and the smell of suspense in the air.
Left alone with my lace-covered curves
and carnivorous thoughts.

Lady Poe

She's the chill of what's to come and a dash of Lady Poe,
with thoughts as dark as violets
and moonlight raining from her soul.

Mortal Queens

Some women wear their darkness so beautifully,
it's easy to forget they're mortal.
Dressed in black silk gowns instead of ballroom gowns
while turning men into wild horses at midnight.

When She's Ready

Where do I find a girl like that?
Oh baby, you don't.
She'll come when she's ready...
cooing, commanding
and dripping in love spells.

Red Wine & Madness

To the *Goddesses* whose veins flow with potions
and red wine;
backs adorned in feathered gowns and elegant madness;
whose magic wands come draped in strength,
sacrifice and sorrow.
I recognize you...

Feral

Her heart is a home for feral things.
Things that bite and things that roam.
Full of gems and a few jagged stones.
Loving, alone, atop her throne.

Come to me

She wasn't a demanding woman.
She just wanted her men to come when she called.
Delirious off devotion
and the smell of magic in the air,
they always did.

Those Howls

Baby, that's not her temper...
it's her wolves howling.
She beats to the rhythm of her own sensual drum;
arousing, inspiring and ever so deeply disturbing
the demons that lie in wait with bated breath.
And in this tale of fairies and fires
anxiously awaiting the kiss of her flame,
she's defiantly both the drug and the fix.

Creatures from the Wicked Lagoon

Women are wondrous, wicked creatures.
Crazy in love with you one moment;
putting a curse on you the next.

All the Dark Feels

She's...
dripping candles,
black tulips
and
cold kisses.
Not just the dark poem,
but the whole haunted bookshop.

Unapologetic

Delicate, beautifully destructive &
unapologetically drunk on darkness.
I desire dark spells that match the mood of my lover;
clouds that cry and the
sounds of thunder and sighs
that come to visit him and I
in the middle of the night.
Poetic highs and his magic eyes...
eyes made just for me.

Half & Half

She's half magic; half monster
rose-red cloaked pixie; raven-gowned witch;
forest cottage covered in alluring flowers;
Gothic castle guarded by ancient statues;
rough edges; silk curves;
the bee dripping honey
and the wasp that stings.

Moody Melodies

You don't have to explain to anyone
the rhythms of your
moods
melodies
and magic spells.
Let them swing and sway
in a beautifully soft, stinging, strange way.

𝕳ome

And some of us are born with souls so dark,
even the crows make a home there.
At night, a creeping vigil of fluttering melancholia.
By morning, an arrival of flapping, fierce wings.

That Place

In that otherworldly place of the early morning hours
where the light and lavender play,
you will find your demons,
dreams
and desires.

The Way She Loved

She didn't love with all her heart.
She loved from the deepest, darkest caves of her soul,
where serpents lie in wait;
butterflies adorn their black wings,
and creeping vines stake their claim.

That Magical Love

And there are some women with souls so old,
they refuse to settle for anything less than
deep, dusky, magical love.
The kind so maddening and murky,
ordinary just won't do.

Hungry Dancers

Her soul is a gathering place for unique,
breathtaking oddities.
Soft madness upon famished lips that
wish to feast;
sordid intimacy
and shadows yearning for hungry dancers.
A witch's curse versus a fairytale
And a monster who gets spoon fed in the end.

Venomous

I like my headdress veiled in
venomous florals;
the way my desires dance on the
edge of darkness,
and his hand possessing the small of my back
as his words crawl up the curve of my spine.

Battle Scars

My heart has always had a sweet tooth
for tombstones and blood-stained euphoria.
Lovers laced in black orchids,
battle scars
and pretty words from afar.

Forever

She'll forever be a girl in love with
inked hearts,
old souls,
antique eyes
and secrets untold.

Read to Me

When I asked him for love letters
he read to me Gothic literature by way of magic spells
and smoldering eye contact,
while Emily & Edgar looked on in pleasure.

Spell Casters

Black hearts don't break.
They cast spells, fill their poetic wells
and never, ever forget.
And while the silk bed sheets run cold,
and her sorrow slips into smoldering intent,
the church bells and headstones begin to make eye contact.

Wishing

Always wishing for a little quiet, a little rest
and the company of dark skies that sing lullabies
to the beautiful unrest in my soul.

In Love

Just a girl who loves things from long ago
watching her poison flower pots grow,
curling up at night,
under candlelight,
to be seduced by
dark love songs
and to feast upon the darkness of his soul.

Dear Dracula

Tonight, I've left my window open
despite the weather being bad.
Neverland was full of lost boys
and Wonderland is mad.
Edgar has been keeping me company,
but he continues to be lonely and sad.
If you can oblige me a caped adventure
with a little teeth and tongue,
I'll be sure to leave the lights off
and my neck reverently unclad.

Yours truly,
Ann Marie

Pretty Mess

She's a messy, moody, maddening
darker shade of magic.
You'll find her with blackbirds in her hair,
a pen in one hand and a wand in the other...
creating temptation as she goes.

True Goddesses

A true Goddess won't speak poorly behind your back.
If you wrong her, she will tell you
in the prowl of her actions,
the measure of her mood,
and the madness in her eyes.

Tis Magical

It's magical what a day of solitude
on a rainy day
in your own space
surrounded by your favorite things
can do for your soul.

They Will Tell Stories About Her

And one day, they will tell stories about her.
A tempest; a strange, ethereal creature
who sought love in darkness,
and kept diaries with the moon.
She left behind the scent of solitude,
and made lone wolves cry.
Sometimes, when night settles in,
you can still hear her wings playing tag with the sky.

Lost and Found

Alice doesn't want to be lost,
and the White Rabbit isn't the decoy.
Sometimes, he lures you into madness.
and all you can do is follow.

𝕱𝖎𝖓𝖉 𝕸𝖊 𝕬 𝕸𝖆𝖓

Find me a man who can walk through my haunted forest,
embrace my fighting limbs
and eat my poison apples,
and I will show him
what a girl on the dark side of a fairytale can do.

Where She Will Be

You'll find her amongst the black roses;
between the pages of Sylvia's words
humming mad songs and
making friends with the midnight birds.

Exquisite

There is a part of me I keep under lock and key.
It wanders into dark, enchanted places
and never comes back alone.
Staggering in torn silk and secrets.
Playful, witch-like, an exquisite combination
of gangster and goddess.
Drenched in veiled allurement.

Rose

A rose is still a rose...
monster,
lust,
fairy dust
and all.

Weeping Elegance

Some wear their crowns so elegantly,
it's easy to forget the weeping horns
and bleeding thorns
that reside beneath.

Lady Lava

Ladylike
but full of
lust
&
lava.

Lulled to Sleep

Her soul is a bewitching shade of dark.
The kind that awakened the beast in gentle men
and lulled the stars to sleep.

Queen

She hustles in her halo and sleeps in her horns
Tastes like sugar, sharp as thorns
Walks with sass and loves with a whole lot of badass
She holds down her friends and buries her foes
Sly as a fox and smart as a crow
Gracious as a princess, strong as a queen
A bit of heaven, a dash of hell and everything in between.

My Intuition

My intuition doesn't speak in whispers and tugs.
It seeps in my way of scorned screeching crows,
the shrill cry of forlorn mermaids
and the harsh tapping of moth wings against my windows
in the dead of night.

Sonnets

Don't give me your average love affair.
I want dark, mad and magical.
Black pearls strung across my neck,
men with midnight eyes
and nights filled with secrets, sonnets and sin.

Hearts on Ice

Women like her wore their hearts on ice
and their souls on their sleeves...
adoring,
addictive
and so very inviting.

Torrential

Love my madness, my moodiness
and my full moons.
Dance with my darkness, my demons
and their mistresses.
Hum to my temper, my tantrums
and my torrential downpours.
Whisper to my wanton desires,
my wicked winds and my wild roses.
Or...
Leave me alone.

Nesting

Her nest is her sacred place of sanctuary and rest.
It holds pretty things, secrets and her closet full of wings.
Only those worthy can savor her scent; a beast,
a Rhett Butler or a dark-blooded gent.
He needs to love her and know his way around her dark;
someone who knows when to playfully nip
and when it's time to bark.

His Howls

If his eyes don't tell you how he feels,
the smell of his skin
and the way he howls
your name at eventide will.
Like a moonflower in love...

Power Tears

Some little girls grow up
and turn their tears,
fears
and rabbit holes of hell into
power,
poetry and golden spells.

Lovely Messes

Give me a moody mess of a man with singing scars and the
echo of my pulse beating in his neck.
Give me dirty and delicious.
Give me real and raw.
Give me loyal liquid lava that fuels my love and madness.
Give me soul-sobbing stares.
Give me dark, inky depth.
Give me him.

Tones

Sometimes darkness comes wrapped in the
hushed,
blushing tones
of the prettiest souls.

𝕳𝖊𝖆𝖛𝖞 𝕳𝖆𝖓𝖉𝖘

How I wanted him...
his kisses, his hisses and the way his
heavy hands gripped my dark, dancing hips.

Dark Despair

There is something to be said about a man
who unites with a woman's
dragons,
darkness,
desires
& despairs.

Amber

She's all...
Amber eyes,
cloudy skies
and
thoughts that make grown men cry.
She'll take you to dark, hidden places
where not many roam.
Where the crows tell their secrets
and needful hearts bare their souls.

Dancing Souls

Beware the girls with souls full of
dancing moons, onyx spoons
and monsters with pretty eyes.

Poetic Spells

Give me those poetic spells and midnight swells
that stir mating calls and perfume the night air
with unholy admissions.
The kind of dark love we don't talk about
when the sun comes up.

Be You

Never be afraid to blossom into the
flower you were meant to be...
strange or silk,
black belladonna or blush rose,
elegant or eerie,
or a majestic blend of all.
Be you.
Wonderfully, magically, you.

Secret Ingredient

I told him I grow in darkness.
He said he had the secret ingredients for the
perfect moonlit garden.

Loyal Rings

Forget the Prince Charmings and the handsome kings...
I want a loyal dragon and a pair of wings,
to take me away from fakes,
fools
and frogs with dirty wedding rings.

Leave Her Lost

Alice didn't want to be saved.
She wanted to live amongst the lost, mad and imaginary.
Some girls don't wish to be found.

Torment

'tis such sweet torment to be possessed
by a ravenous,
yet tender heart.

Broken

We're all a little broken.
We all have a little strange magic.
Dance with it.
Bring it flowers.
Bring it tea,
and let your darkness have a sip.
It's the secret ingredient
to some of our best remedies.

Thunderclouds

He's all black mist and a midnight kiss...
and the thunderclouds
that roar between my hips.

Aloof

Oh, to be an aloof, solitary maiden
in a world full of social butterflies.
I used to feel badly about that,
but now I rejoice.
Reveling in my time alone,
as I turn my wand into my voice.

White Rabbit

Darling girl,
Follow that white rabbit
and fuck what they say.

Tempers

And then there are those with magic tempers,
mouths full of rain water
and the cries of a thousand black cats
beating in their chest.
You know the ones.

Magical Creatures

Women are magical creatures,
with kisses bearing both stars and storms,
and voices colorful enough to put crying babes to sleep
while scaring men to death.

Lure & Lunacy

Beware those magic girls.
They will love you, lure you
and put you in a state of lunacy...
begging for mercy.

Rare is He

Rare is the man who can stay drunk
on her darkness and demons.
Such a welcome scent for the wolves...

Hell Scented

I don't know if there are angels looking over me,
but my demons keep a tight vigil
reminding me every night of the
hell-scented flowers coursing through my veins.

Capture

I was born to capture Prince Charming,
not be rescued by him.
I make no apologies for the sides of me
I only show to those worthy to see...
my dark, my magic dust, my sensual, strange moody spells
that take trips to faraway places.
Oftentimes, getting lost there for days.

Singing Serpents

I love the mystifying,
dark way stormy days move inside me,
rousing my vices and vines...
singing my magic and melodies to life.

Dark Beauty Souls

~Drinking black tea in a Gothic courtyard with Mary Shelley
~Clinging silk gowns
~Chandeliers in every room
~Living next to a haunted cemetery,
in a New England seaside town,
where the night winds sing haunting melodies
~Re-watching "The Ghost and Mrs. Muir" on a rainy day
~Glass vases and antique lockets
filled with black orchids and night tulips
~Reading paranormal romance on a cold night.
~A backyard arboretum, filled with crows,
who watch over me.

Wildfire

Her darkness is no match for wildfire.
It soars on the blackest of wings
and sings stories only a few will understand.

Brunettes

Brunettes are...
sleek thorns,
dark chocolate
and
desire.
And to love her, is to do so
deeply,
daringly
and full of
folly and rain.

𝕳er 𝕻oetry

Her poetry isn't always pen and prose.
Sometimes, its pinning him against the wall
and drinking the words
straight from his lips.

𝔑ight & 𝔇ay

She had that nighttime wild streak...
fire, wildflowers, swan dances full of blush and brimstone,
a mouth full of erotica.
And on quiet, gentle days, she could be found
full of rain, romance novels and a bleeding heart overflowing
in love songs and longing.

𝔐𝔢

Give me a tiny cottage at the edge of the forest
and by the sea,
where it thunders
and rains
and allows me to be me.

Darkly Ever After

He pulled my different out of me...
my sins, my strange,
the restless creatures dangling from my heartstrings.
And, like a bouquet of queens of the night gleaming
in an indigo vase,
and words poured onto a Gothic backdrop,
he enchantingly and elegantly danced me into the pages
of his bedtime story, where we lived darkly ever after.

𝕽𝖊𝖈𝖑𝖚𝖘𝖊

Her butterflies are not delicate, dancing socialites.
They are elusive, black moths in disguise.
Lovers of quiet nights and solitary places.

Ballads

The way to her heart is through sultry ballads
laced upon a loyal lover's tongue
while locking eyes with the Monstress
that resides in her soul.

Restless

Too many white picket fences
and not enough dark castles
cloaked in moats,
lilac groves,
and the voices of restless goddesses.

What I Need

I don't need anymore nightmares or fairytale promises.
I need a gentle beast, with wolf instincts and silky loving lips
who knows when to pet me
and when to pin me against walls.

Mysterious Disguise

Come and play in her pretty, soulful eyes...
sweeping men off their feet with their mysterious disguise;
dancing, dizzy butterflies
and sensual, tear-stained war cries.

Forbidden Things

She loves staying up past her bedtime,
making love and moon bathing under a sky full of ravens,
clouds the color of ruby slippers,
and the whisper of dark and forbidden things.
Nighttime is her favorite time.

Lily & Lioness

Some days I'm the lily
and others, the lioness.
And sometimes, I let my wicked bitch out to play
to remind myself I've got this
and it's all going to be okay.

Strange Storms

She's always been a little strange, stormy...
singing to the tune of her own love song.
And she wouldn't have it any other way.

Euphoria

I used to fear the demons that resided inside my lover's soul,
but now they're the first I get to know
to ensure they are worthy of my euphoria,
my everlasting fire
and the secrets that reside deep within my rabbit hole.

Remedies & Poison

Sometimes its not the remedy that saves you,
but her poison and the way she
wears her monsters just as pretty
as her midnight secrets
and morning gowns.

Soft & Sensual

She wants it soft and sensual,
savage and seductive.
Her hauntingly quaint soul will love you,
enchant you,
leave you breathless and bewitched
as it tucks you into her side of the bed with her wolves.

Solitary Raven

I'll always be a secluded, shrill raven
amongst the clusters of singing songbirds.

My Darkness

Some days my darkness wraps me in cloaks
and reminds me who I'm dealing with.
Other days, it gets on its knees and calls me Queen.

Deep Wells

In those deep wells of stormy days is where you'll find her
dancing with her demons and covered in ink.
The place she keeps her treasured things,
her secrets and thoughts,
and keepsake box full of black wings.

Cinderella

My Cinderella would have preferred the pumpkins.
The quiet little attic room with trinkets in jars,
and candlelit nooks for writing.
No crowded balls or fancy glass,
or rooms too big to breathe.
Just her man with a sword,
her hair let down
and her loyal little creatures at her feet.

If By Date You Mean,

~strolling through used bookstores;
~having a picnic in a quiet, enchanted forest
while collecting dead leaves;
~wandering through an old, Gothic cemetery;
~house hunting in a haunted, coastal town
as the crows look on;
~happening upon a portal to a dark,
magical otherworldly place,
then yes, let's go.

Ornamental Attics

She always had a love of beautiful, dark things;
ghost stories, ornamental attics
and the sound of a night sky full of raven wings.
Antique silk spun with many a lover's tear,
names like Isidora and Aurora,
and his words delivering ice hot chills
from her shoulder, to her nape, to her ear.

Spells

Some of the softest women
possess the most powerful spells.
We weren't meant to sit silent and pretty.
We were meant to fly to the moon atop
broomsticks and blooming wings
with pockets full of poppies and curses.
Leading packs while singing poetry.
Crashing parties in raven-colored cloaks
as we bear gifts and recite cradle songs.
That is what we were made for.

Arsenic & Old Lace

She has a heart brimming in arsenic
and a soul gracefully lined with old lace.
A classic queen; a starry-eyed soul
full of seduction and super moons.
Draped in antiques and ancient ruins,
singing songs of centuries ago.
Her secret self will forever long for an
old-fashioned lull in a modern, noisy world.

𝔐𝔦𝔯𝔯𝔬𝔯 𝔐𝔦𝔯𝔯𝔬𝔯 𝔬𝔫 𝔱𝔥𝔢 𝔚𝔞𝔩𝔩

That pretty mirror on the wall...
at times the starlet, nectar and all.
But restless days bring the games out to play...
temptress, fire queen, lovers and prey.

Lady Lovers

Those soft, lady lovers
feeling like luxurious lace, every day enchantresses...
lustful, wicked fairies at nightfall.
Ever so rare, once in a lifetime finds.

Land of Misfit Toys

I'll forever be a loner, a solitary queen.
Always wanting to be heard through my words,
but comfortable not being seen.
A lover of uniquely blended strangeness,
beasts and black sheep boys.
Forever where my heart will roam in the land of misfit toys.

Longs To Be

Once upon a poem
is where she longs to be.
Flying with the ravens
above wildflowers,
storms
& ghostly seas.

Feral Birds

My heart beats to the sound of feral birds in flight
and the way they say my name
like a plea and a prayer.
Sometimes begging...sometimes taking.

Wary Souls

It takes a special someone to love a girl with a wary soul;
skeletons that hold deep secrets and sorrows,
and snapdragons rooted with so much grace and deceit,
they ask her permission to grow.

Silk Gowns

Her mind loves to dress in silk gowns
and chase pretty words...
ethereal, alluring, enchanting, celestial, spellbinding.

While her soul longs to dance with the darker side of his...
brooding, moody, haunting, feral, hungry.

Her heart bleeds for both and awaits with eager eyes.

To Tend & Guard

Primrose on the outside tended by fairies.
Primal on the inside guarded by fire.

Never trample her garden or anger her nesting dragon.

Nesting Kind of Girl

I'm an abandoned castle loving
cathedral exploring
antique store strolling
New England bookshop browsing
cemetery obsessing
forest nesting kind of girl.

Dripping Romance

Her heart is full of dark moods
and the dead silence of the forest
in the middle of the night.
But her love...
Her love is ravenous, molten
And romance dripping in flame-tipped madness.

𝕱𝖗𝖔𝖑𝖎𝖈 & 𝕱𝖗𝖊𝖓𝖈𝖍 𝕶𝖎𝖘𝖘

Don't promise me with trips to hell
for the way my sins choose to frolic and French kiss.
I've seen your handbasket and the way your angels
look longingly at my display of impish ornaments.
I'd rather play with the sinners
than pretty up the evidence with the saints.

Antique Tea Cups

My antique tea cup is but half full
of Pandora's curses & nestling madness;
part weeping willow, part wicked witch.
My soul settled upon a dark, enchanting castle
above the cold sea,
while my heart tugs for seeping, howling things.

Things that Cling

A lady like her doesn't scare easily.
She's been playing in fields of clovers
and calla lilies since she was a girl.
More pretty in poison than pretty in pink.
Befriending things that cling and dark downy eyes.

Pinky Promises

I could tell you my secrets,
but then my demons would have to get involved
and they don't do well with pinky promises.

Dates with Death

She's more than the mask she wears
to protect herself from dates with death
and the promise of dead roses.
You'll find her cloaked unmercifully
in goddess-scented gowns
and walls of wisteria as they come begging for forgiveness
and a chance to fall in love.

Dark Rain

Maybe if we'd had less deceiving sunny days
& more tastes of dark rain;
less black and white & more enchantments and gray...
encouraged to dance with our temper-laced tears,
instead of tsk'd for our pain,
we'd all be a little more okay.

Obsidian Depths

He came intending to splash and skinny-dip in my
well of obsidian depths,
only to find himself submerged in the sweet scent of my
scorn and scars...
Never to surface again.

The Way She Wore It

She wore armor of brimstone & black lace.
In sync with eerie things...
menacing, untamed and taboo.
Things that go bump in the night
and take flight
upon black wings
and thoughts not of this world.

Bewitching Belle

Bewitching as the beauty who sleeps,
Sinful as her foreshadowing horns.
Belle-like in poetic reverie,
prickly as her shapely thorns.

Playful Banter

Blessed with a vintage soul, a burning heart
and a wicked mouth that loves to tease
and test rough waters.
They love to banter and bet one another,
but when they join forces,
they always get what they want.

Drown Him

He was intrigued by my dark, murky depths.
Wondering if I was going to join him in the deep end
or drown him.

178

Nothing More

Sometimes those pretty love letters
are nothing more than
black magic spells.
You see, I have a habit of falling
for dark, luxurious types.
The ones who lavish me with borrowed scripts
and a belly full of fluttering bats
that slowly devour my heart.

Fireflies

Tell the fireflies I've arrived.
It's time to dance
and fill our diaries with dirty poetry.

Blackened Hearts

I like my lover's heart blackened,
a haven of paradise and purgatory,
where the ravens and I can rest in peace.

Soft Leather

I never let anyone explore my darkness
until he came along...
adorned in magic,
leather
and
soft lips.

Freshly Bathed

Many a night I stayed up late
praying and pleading with my angels.
But it was always my jewelry box of cimmerian treasures,
freshly bathed and with a brave face,
greeting me come morning.

Black Diamonds

He was so good at feeding me his sins.
And I, master at turning them into
burning embers
and
black diamonds.

The Mender

Some women mend the crowns of other women
reminding them of both the
beauty and the beast
residing within.
Others try to knock the crown off
and steal the jewels.
Be the beautiful mender.

What She Needed

And when the angels didn't come for her,
the darkness did,
for it knew exactly what she needed.

Ominous Places

Her shadows have a life of their own
and sometimes take her to places even the crows
don't dare land.

Green with Envy

Be careful with her.
The fairytale is dark,
her ghosts are green with envy,
and her demons don't take kindly to sharing.

Darkened Depths

Don't be afraid to drown in her darkened depths.
It's the most beautiful place to be
lost,
found
and loved forever.

𝕻𝖗𝖊𝖙𝖙𝖞 𝕻𝖔𝖈𝖐𝖊𝖙𝖘

She reads like an Anne Rice novel,
but feels like silk against sinuous curves.
Tenderness and hungry teeth.
A soft-hearted lover with pockets full of opium poppies.

Dark Skies

I've never been one to wait for the sun to come out.
I linger for dark skies
and the end of the day to arrive.
Hushed corners that hug me and nighttime thoughts that
creep out of their hiding place.

Let's Play

I dared him to come play in my dark...
he double dared me to come along and watch.

Where She Finds Comfort

Her soul, ever bathed in darkness,
finds comfort in hearts housed in mausoleums,
the sinister stories of dark red queens,
and in his arms, where there lie the softest thorns
and secrets meant only for her.

Lily and Morticia

I grew up grasping the hemlines of Lily and Morticia,
following them through their macabre, magical mansions.
They showed me how midnight cravings grow
and how dark queens blossom
from seedlings carefully sowed...
unapologetic, powerful and painted
in the prettiest shades
of the full moon.

Lunacy & Lovers

If you find her in the dark,
leave her be.
It's the only time she can let her lunacy & lovers out to play.

Primal Desires

I'll always crave adoration and romance;
languorous kisses and sultry softness.
But like air to breathe,
I'll forever need his primal desires
gripping me by hip and hair,
while we bathe each other in the deepest, darkest parts of
our souls.

Amethyst Maiden

She's...
Melancholy songbirds,
ancient skeleton secrets
and
the amethyst maiden who lovingly
bathes the sky at twilight.
Sitting atop a forest tree, with her cape and black tea
sharing poetry and stories with sage souls.

Salvation

Sometimes a woman's darkness
is a man's only salvation.
And more often than not,
that's exactly what it needs to be.

Sea Glass

Don't let the lilt of her voice
or her lovely shades of sea glass fool you.
Her sirens are known to swim to the surface
awaiting the poets and dreamers,
and things that come alive in the dead of night.

Hungry Hearts

Women like her don't undress their feelings often.
They're too busy playing house with dark, enchanted things
and keeping time with hungry hearts.

Sunday Morning

I'm not a Sunday morning love song.
I'm that dark romance set in a classic haunting tale;
surrounded by Gothic chandeliers
and handsome suits with devil eyes.
Where devious housekeepers keep notes
and the sky cries in shades of gray
and overgrown graveyards.

Black Cat Tendencies

She makes no apologies for being both
foul-mouthed and fancy-free.
Born a creature of the night
with addictive cravings
and black cat tendencies.

Cover of Darkness

Long after he and I have said our goodnights,
our souls emerge from the shadows,
undress and curl up
under the cover of darkness
to sip on each other's angels,
demons
and
deepest fantasies.

Equal parts

She's equal parts dark damsel & moonflower...
ghostly,
vague,
lush
&
alluring.
A dream within a dream
of places she keeps hidden from the light.

Erotic

Erotic ebbs and flows
and swings and sways.
His beautiful beasts danced behind his eyes,
while soft lips left traces of sin upon my skin.

Jekyll & Hyde

Those Jekyll & Hyde types.
They'll come bearing the key to your love chambers,
while your monster begins planning a happily never after.
Unkempt promises spilling from pretty, toxic-laced mouths.

206

Moods & Magic

He's all brooding moods and black magic.
She's all soft temper and poetic spells.
Together, they created potions that made the dark turn red.

Childhood

She grew up left to her own imagination
and the solitude of a magical, haunted little nook
of the Connecticut woods.
There is where the seed of enchanted darkness was planted
and her allure of raven-haired wicked Queens was born.

Whispers of Ravens

You'd find comfort in the dark too
if your soul was wrapped in the whispers of ravens
and the warmth of their wings.

𝕻𝖗𝖊𝖙𝖙𝖞 𝕷𝖎𝖙𝖙𝖑𝖊 𝕾𝖎𝖗𝖊𝖓

She's...
Dark romance,
ill-tempered
&
drips of honey laced with whiskey and want, siren and salt.
They all think they know her
but the eyes can be deceiving.
Raindrops can turn to black lagoons
as staying can turn to leaving.

Beware

Beware the girl with *Wonderland* in her eyes.
Her love sheds both fragrant petals and the potent bristle-
scented scars of her ancestors.
Harm her and the force of her fairy godmother,
wise and versed in the secrets of the blue devil,
will haunt you forever.

Where Her Garden Grows

You'll never see the sun shining upon her gardens,
for that's where the rain,
her lovers
and blackened hearts
bathing under silver stars
have claimed their homes.

Jasmine

She's the Harvest moon,
sultry moods
& the chilling smell of jasmine after dark.
Amongst the brambles and briars,
and the sharpest thorns,
are often the gentlest, rarest beauties
there ever was.

Soul Sprouting

Some days she needs to be alone
while the dark poems sprout from her soul.
Words that sing and thoughts that scream.
Slowing dancing to the edge of darkness
begging for her blades to stay strong.

She Wears Darkness on her Sleeve

Don't let the pretentious ones make you feel
prose should always be graceful lips and pretty words.
For the ones born with darkness on their sleeve
and nighttime in their souls,
know the difference
between an assuming sky full of imaginary sunshine
and a moonlit forest full of pure poetry.

Fair Maiden

Fair Maiden?
No.
A Dark Queen with hypnotic hymns,
a crow's intuition
and pretty, painted claws
that leave marks on her men forever.

Loving Him

And how she loves a man
who knows how to make her darkness
hiss, hum and sigh in relief.
A soothing balm upon her fiery heart.
A chilling arousal to keep her soul his.

Poison Apples

Poison apples and lacy thighs;
sulky lips and dusky eyes.
Skin that glows as the moon herself
and hair as black as midnight skies.
A lover of fairytales dipped in wicked delight,
that made the evil blush and awakened Snow White.

Glass Daisies

And when the clock strikes midnight,
I don't care who's left holding the shoe...
as long as he comes bearing darkness, glass daisies
and the devil's charm,
ready to make me his immortal lover.

Save Us

Sometimes, the princess is really the witch.
The damsel is the dagger
and true love ends up being the beast
who rescues you from both the
prince and the fairytale.

Bitch or Beauty

Give me unexpected, intimate get togethers
surrounded by pretty mad hatters,
the strange and the loyal.
Those I can be myself with, whether bitch or beauty.
Those I don't have to watch my tongue around.
Those who get me.

Magical Lust

That scent before a storm is her
bed of lust and magic,
and the bees who
don't know whether to join in her chaos
or bring her honey.

Midnight Lace

And when her magic and midnight lace come for you,
forsake the thought of resisting.
You won't be able to.
You know it.
I know it.
And she definitely knows it.

ABOUT THE AUTHOR

Ann Marie Eleazer has always considered herself a bit ancient, haunted and otherworldly, who enjoys enchanted flights through the dark fairy tales and magical places she's been drawn to since childhood. What began as a creative outlet, soon became an unleashing of what lies beneath into her world of bewitching darkness and poetic passion. She began sharing her work in 2017, where she accumulated a widespread fan base and her desire to publish her work grew. A lover of all things that beautifully grow in the dark, she enjoys reading, collecting antiques, all things paranormal and filling pages with magic while spending time at her home, in the woods, with her family and furbabies.

Discover more from Author Ann Marie Eleazer at:

Facebook: facebook.com/shesmagicandmidnightlace
Instagram: instagram.com/shesmagicandmidnightlace_
Pinterest: pinterest.com/aeleazer2317
Twitter: twitter.com/she_midnight